D09938518

SPINOSAURUS

BY SUSAN H. GRAY · ILLUSTRATED BY ROBERT SQUIER

The Child's World

Published in the United States of America by The Child's World®
1980 Lookout Drive • Mankato, MN 56003-1705
800-599-READ • www.childsworld.com

ACKNOWLEDGMENTS
The Child's World®: Mary Berendes, Publishing Director
The Design Lab: Kathleen Petelinsek, Art Direction and Design;
Victoria Stanley and Anna Petelinsek, Page Production
Editorial Directions: E. Russell Primm, Editor; Lucia Raatma, Copy Editor;
Dina Rubin, Proofreader; Tim Griffin, Indexer

PHOTO CREDITS
©Jhunnius/Dreamstime.com: cover, 2–3; ©University of Pennsylvania
Gazette, July/August 2001, and Paläontologisches Museum München: 7;
©Jonathan Blair/Corbis: 12–13; ©Rick Ergenbright/Corbis: 16–17; ©the
Granger Papers Project: 18–19, 19 (right)

LIBRARY OF CONGRESS CATALOGING-IN-PUBLICATION DATA
Gray, Susan Heinrichs.
 Spinosaurus / by Susan H. Gray; Illustrated by Robert Squier.
    p. cm.—(Introducing dinosaurs)
 Includes bibliographical references and index.
 ISBN 978-1-60253-241-0 (lib. bound: alk. paper)
 1. Spinosaurus—Juvenile literature. I. Squier, Robert, ill. II. Title. III. Series.
 QE862.S3G69562 2009
 567.912—dc22   2009001628

TABLE OF CONTENTS

WHAT WAS SPINOSAURUS?

Spinosaurus (spy-no-SAWR-uss) was an enormous dinosaur. It lived millions of years ago. Its name means "spiny **lizard**." *Spinosaurus* had a row of spines along its back. A sheet of skin connected the spines. Together, the skin and spines formed a sail.

A number of dinosaurs had sails on their backs.
Spinosaurus *was the largest of them.*

6

WHAT DID *SPINOSAURUS* LOOK LIKE?

Spinosaurus was gigantic. It weighed more than two cars. It walked around on two huge legs. The head of *Spinosaurus* was as long as a bathtub. The mouth was filled with sharp teeth.

Spinosaurus also had a magnificent sail. It was 6 feet (1.8 meters) tall in the middle. That's as tall as a grown-up person!

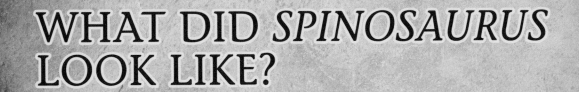

Spinosaurus *was very big, even for a dinosaur. Just one bone could be almost as tall as a person!*

WHAT WAS THAT SAIL FOR?

No one knows why *Spinosaurus* had that big sail. Maybe it helped *Spinosaurus* to have the right **temperature**. If dinosaurs got too cold, they could not move very fast. If they got too hot, their bodies might overheat.

We are still trying to learn why Spinosaurus *had a sail on its back. One day, we might find the answer.*

On cold days, maybe *Spinosaurus* stood out in the sun. The sail caught the sun's rays. Then *Spinosaurus* warmed up. On hot days, maybe *Spinosaurus* stood in the shade. Breezes blew against the sail. Then *Spinosaurus* cooled down.

We can only guess how Spinosaurus *used its sail. Some people believe that it used the sail to control its body temperature.*

WHAT DID *SPINOSAURUS* DO ALL DAY?

Spinosaurus probably spent lots of time eating and sleeping. **Scientists** think that *Spinosaurus* ate fish. It stood by a lake and stared into the water. Then it snapped up a fish and swallowed it whole.

This fish would have been a tasty meal for Spinosaurus.

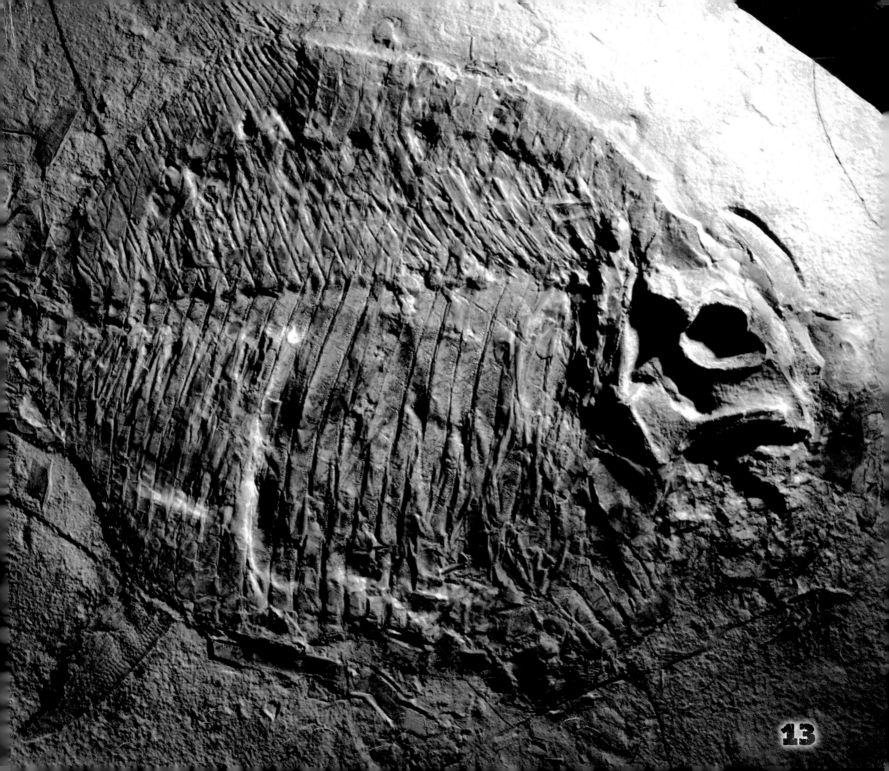

Perhaps *Spinosaurus* also hunted other dinosaurs. Or maybe it ate animals that were already dead. A hungry *Spinosaurus* probably was not a picky eater!

Spinosaurus *was big enough to eat smaller dinosaurs. With a gulp,* Spinosaurus *would have a quick meal.*

HOW DO WE KNOW ABOUT *SPINOSAURUS?*

Most dinosaurs just rotted away after they died. Sometimes their bones were preserved by nature. They were buried in **sandstorms** or on lake bottoms. The bones stayed there for years and turned into **fossils**.

Scientists continue to look for new Spinosaurus *fossils. Many of these fossils are found in Africa.*

Years ago, scientists found *Spinosaurus* fossils in Africa. They found teeth, **skull** bones, and long spines. What a discovery! Now we know about *Spinosaurus*.

Richard Markgraf (left) was the first scientist to find Spinosaurus fossils. Fossil hunters have been searching for bones in Africa for many years (above).

WHERE HAVE SPINOSAURUS BONES BEEN FOUND?

Tunisia

Egypt

Niger

NORTH AMERICA

Atlantic Ocean

Pacific Ocean

EUROPE

ASIA

AFRICA

SOUTH AMERICA

Indian Ocean

AUSTRALIA

Map Key

Where *Spinosaurus* bones have been found

Southern Ocean

WHO FINDS THE BONES?

Fossil hunters find dinosaur bones. Some fossil hunters are scientists. Others are people who hunt fossils for fun. They go to areas where dinosaurs once lived. They find bones in rocky places, in mountainsides, and in deserts.

When fossil hunters discover dinosaur bones, they get busy. They use picks to chip rocks away from the fossils. They use small brushes to sweep off any dirt. They take pictures of the fossils. They also write notes about where the fossils were found. They want to remember everything!

Fossil hunters use many tools to dig up fossils. It is very important to use the right tools so the fossils do not get damaged.

GLOSSARY

fossils (*FOSS-ullz*) Fossils are preserved parts of plants and animals that died long ago.

lizard (*LIZ-urd*) A lizard is a scaly animal that walks on four legs.

sandstorms (*SAND-stormz*) Sandstorms are windy storms that whip sand and dust into the sky.

scientists (*SY-un-tists*) Scientists are people who study how things work through observations and experiments.

skull (*SKUHL*) The skull is the set of bones in the head.

Spinosaurus (*spy-no-SAWR-uss*) *Spinosaurus* was a dinosaur that had spines and a sail on its back.

temperature (*TEM-pur-ah-chur*) The temperature of something is a measurement of how hot or cold it is.

BOOKS

Birch, Robin. *Meat-eating Dinosaurs.*
New York: Chelsea House Publishers, 2008.

Gray, Susan H. *Spinosaurus.* Mankato, MN:
The Child's World, 2005.

Nussbaum, Ben. *Spinosaurus in the Storm.*
Norwalk, CT: Soundprints, 2005.

Parker, Steve. *Dinosaurus: The Complete Guide to Dinosaurs.*
New York: Firefly Books, 2003.

WEB SITES

Visit our Web site for lots of links about *Spinosaurus*:

CHILDSWORLD.COM/LINKS

Note to Parents, Teachers, and Librarians: We routinely verify our Web links to make sure they are safe, active sites—so encourage your readers to check them out!

INDEX

ABOUT THE AUTHOR

Susan Gray has written more than ninety books for children. She especially likes to write about animals. Susan lives in Cabot, Arkansas, with her husband, Michael, and many pets.

ABOUT THE ILLUSTRATOR

Robert Squier has been drawing dinosaurs ever since he could hold a crayon. Today, instead of using crayons, he uses pencils, paint, and the computer. Robert lives in New Hampshire with his wife, Jessica, and a house full of dinosaur toys. *Stegosaurus* is his favorite dinosaur.